First Aid and Emergencies

LIFE SKILLS

First Aid and Emergencies

Published by
Heron Books, Inc.
20950 SW Rock Creek Road
Sheridan, OR 97378

heronbooks.com

Special thanks to all the teachers and students who
provided feedback instrumental to this edition.

Fourth Edition © 1993, 2023 Heron Books.
All Rights Reserved

ISBN: 978-0-89-739340-9

Any unauthorized copying, translation, duplication or distribution, in whole
or in part, by any means, including electronic copying, storage or transmission,
is a violation of applicable laws.

The Heron Books name and the heron bird symbol are registered trademarks
of Delphi Schools, Inc.

1 July 2023

At Heron Books, we think learning should be engaging and fun. It should be hands-on and allow students to move at their own pace.

To facilitate this we have created a learning guide that will help any student progress through this book, chapter by chapter, with confidence and interest.

Get learning guides at
heronbooks.com/learningguides.

For teacher resources,
such as a final exam, email
teacherresources@heronbooks.com.

We would love to hear from you!
Email us at *feedback@heronbooks.com*.

IN THIS BOOK

CHAPTER 1
What is First Aid? 1

CHAPTER 2
Minor Wounds and Bleeding 3
    Infection 4
    Special Note on Bleeding 5
    Handling Minor Wounds 6
    Puncture Wounds 9
    Handling Puncture Wounds 10

CHAPTER 3
Minor Burns 11
    Handling Minor Burns 12

CHAPTER 4
Stings and Bites 13
    Insect Stings 13
    Handling Insect Stings 14
    Bites 15
    Handling Bites 17

CHAPTER 5
Something in the Eye 19
    Handling Something in the Eye 20

CHAPTER 6
Skin Poisoning from Plants 21
Handling Skin Poisoning from Plants 22

CHAPTER 7
Sprains 23
Handling Sprains 24

CHAPTER 8
Heat Emergencies 25
Heat Exhaustion 25
Heat Stroke 26
Handling Heat Emergencies 28

CHAPTER 9
Cold Emergencies 31
Frostbite 31
Hypothermia 32
Handling Cold Emergencies 34

CHAPTER 10
Choking 37
Handling Choking 39

CHAPTER 11
Fainting and Blows to the Head 41
Fainting 41
Handling Fainting 42
Blows to the Head 43
Handling a Blow to the Head 44

CHAPTER 12
Shock 45
Handling Shock 46

CHAPTER 13
Making an Emergency Phone Call 47
Let's Do This: Practice Emergency Phone Calls 49
Let's Do This: Practice Your First Aid 52

CHAPTER 14
Emergencies in the Environment 53

CHAPTER 15
Electrical Emergencies 55
Handling Electrical Emergencies 57

CHAPTER 16
Fire Emergencies 61
How to Put Out Small Fires 62
Using Fire Extinguishers 64
Fire Emergency Plan 66
Handling Fire Emergencies 67
Building on Fire 71

CHAPTER 17
Water Emergencies 75
Handling Water Emergencies 77

CHAPTER 18
Emergencies in Nature 79
Tornados 80
Handling Tornado Emergencies 81

Earthquakes...83
    Handling Earthquake Emergencies 84
Floods...87
    Handling Flood Emergencies............................. 87
Thunderstorms 88
    Handling Thunderstorm Emergencies 89
Let's Do This: Practice Handling Emergencies in the Environment . . 90

Drill Sheet for First Aid 91

Wounds and Bleeding 91
Minor Burns 96
Insect Stings and Bites......................................97
Something in the Eye 99
Skin Poisoning from Plants 100
Sprains..101
Heat Emergencies 102
Cold Emergencies 104
Choking...106
Fainting, Blow to the Head 108
Shock..110

Drill Sheet for Handling Emergencies in the Environment 111

Electrical Emergencies....................................111
Fire Emergencies 113
Building on Fire 116
Water Emergencies 118
Emergencies in Nature 120

CHAPTER 1

What is First Aid?

Aid is help. **First aid** is *emergency* medical help, the help that is given *first* when a person is sick or injured, before they can get full medical help.

When someone needs first aid, you might think that you could just call the emergency help line to find out what to do. Or a nearby adult could fix it. But there might be times when a person needs help before you can call, when there is no adult around, and even times when there is no phone or phone service.

If you know first aid, you can help a sick or injured person who cannot get other medical attention right away.

For example, if you know how to help someone who is choking, you could possibly save their life. They might still need to see a doctor to fully recover, but you would have handled the emergency.

A few other things that first aid can help with are knife cuts, bumped heads, sprained ankles, insect bites, and burns.

WHAT IS FIRST AID?

You can come across many types of injuries, some requiring more aid than you are able to give. This book will tell you about some of the common injuries you might have to deal with, and the first aid steps you would be able to take.

Remember, *first* aid is emergency help given **first**. When you have learned some simple things about giving first aid, you will know what to do if someone around you is hurt or sick and needs fast help.

You can make a big difference!

CHAPTER 2

Minor Wounds and Bleeding

A **wound** is an injury where some part of the body is cut or hurt in way that usually causes some bleeding. A minor wound is one that does not cause a lot of bleeding or damage but still needs to be handled. Examples might be a skinned knee or a cut finger.

The first thing to know about when handling a wound is germs. **Germs** are small, living things that might get into the wound and start attacking that part of the person's body. So, keeping a wound clean is an important part of first aid. To help with this, you should always wash your hands before helping the person.

Minor wounds usually stop bleeding by themselves and just need to be washed, and covered with a bandage.

To clean the wound, rinse it with water. Wash around the wound with soap.

MINOR WOUNDS AND BLEEDING

If you can, it is good to use antibiotic ointment also. Something that is **antibiotic** kills germs. So putting an antibiotic ointment on a wound before putting the bandage over it will help kill germs.

Use a **sterile bandage**. A sterile bandage is specially made to be germ-free. Small ones, like Band-Aids® usually have sticky parts to hold the soft material over the wound.

INFECTION

If germs do get into a wound and start attacking that part of the person's body, this is called an **infection**.

Germs are around us all the time but our bodies can usually fight off and kill enough germs to keep them from causing a problem. But sometimes the germs in a wound "win" for a while, and a wound gets infected. This is why an important part of first aid is getting a wound very clean so this doesn't happen in the first place.

If a wound does get infected, it's a good idea to get some medical attention.

Here's how to spot a wound that is getting infected:

- At first the skin around the wound gets a bit red, puffy and even sorer. **Pus** may form. This is the yellowish, thick liquid that oozes from a wound or is trapped inside a wound.

- If the infection gets worse, the skin around it gets much redder, and swollen, and quite painful.

- An infection can make a person feel ill, possibly even giving them a fever.

MINOR WOUNDS AND BLEEDING

- An infection that has been left alone too long can even spread through the blood, and red streaks can be seen on the body going out from the wound.

If you use good first aid, most minor wounds will heal just fine. But you should be alert for signs of infection, and if you see them, get medical help.

SPECIAL NOTE ON BLEEDING

Be careful not to get another person's blood on your own hands, because you can get a disease more easily that way. If available, wear disposable gloves. If gloves are not available, place some other barrier between the blood and your hands. A clean plastic bag might work well. And *always* wash your own hands well after you give first aid to someone who is bleeding, even if you wear gloves.

MINOR WOUNDS AND BLEEDING

HANDLING MINOR WOUNDS

Situation:

Person has a small wound or scratch with little bleeding.

First Aid:

- Put on disposable gloves or something else as a barrier.

- Clean out of the wound anything you can see, such as dirt, gravel or other things. Rinse the wound with water, and wash around it with soap and water. Let the skin dry.

- If you have antibiotic ointment, put it on the wound.

- Put on a sterile bandage. If you do not have a bandage and the wound is small, you could leave it uncovered.

- Afterward, wash your hands well with hot water and soap.

- If the wound was dirty, have the injured person watch out for infection, and get medical attention if needed.

MINOR WOUNDS AND BLEEDING

Situation:

Person has a wound or cut, and the bleeding does not stop right away.

First Aid:

- Put on disposable gloves or something else to cover your hands.

- Cover the wound with a sterile bandage, or a clean pad or cloth if a bandage isn't available.

- Have the injured person press hard enough to stop the blood flow, or if they can't, do it yourself.

- If the wound is on an arm or leg and the bleeding doesn't stop quickly, raise the arm or leg above the level of the heart. This will help stop the bleeding faster.

- After the bleeding has stopped, put on a new sterile bandage.

- Afterward, wash your hands well with hot water and soap.

- If it's a larger wound, have the injured person get immediate medical attention.

MINOR WOUNDS AND BLEEDING

Situation:

Person has a nosebleed.

A **nosebleed** is a small wound inside the nose. Because the bleeding comes from inside the nose, nosebleeds are handled differently than other wounds.

First Aid:

- Put on disposable gloves or something else to cover your hands.

- Have the person sit up, lean forward, breathe through their mouth, and pinch the soft part of their nostrils together (just below the bone) for ten minutes. You can also hold a cold, wet cloth to their nose and face while they are pinching.

- If the bleeding doesn't stop after 10 minutes, pinch it for another 10 minutes.

- The person should not blow their nose for several hours after the bleeding stops.

- Afterward, wash your hands well with hot water and soap.

PUNCTURE WOUNDS

A **puncture** is a hole made by a sharp object. **Puncture wounds** are wounds made by sharp objects such as pins, nails, splinters, stabs, bullets, and even teeth (through animal or people bites).

Puncture wounds are often difficult to clean. Puncture wounds usually don't bleed much so germs and dirt aren't carried out by the blood. The sharp object can carry germs into the wound, and they may grow more easily in the deeper wound.

Puncture wounds are more dangerous than what are called "open" wounds because the skin tends to close over the wound. This can trap germs inside, where they can't be cleaned out, and the wound doesn't heal well.

One of the germs that can get inside the body from a puncture wound can cause a serious disease called tetanus. **Tetanus** causes an extreme stiffness of some muscles, especially those that control the jaw. There are shots that protect people from tetanus germs. The medical recommendation is that if a person gets a puncture wound and hasn't ever had a tetanus shot, or if it has been many years since their last shot, they should see their doctor right away.

MINOR WOUNDS AND BLEEDING

HANDLING PUNCTURE WOUNDS

Situation:

Person has a puncture wound with little bleeding (for example, stepped on a nail or a large splinter).

First Aid:

- Put on disposable gloves or something else as a barrier.

- Clean out of the wound anything you can see, such as dirt, gravel or other things. Then gently press around the wound to help it bleed. Getting any blood or pus out of the wound may help clean it.

- Wash the wound well with soap and water.

- Put on antibiotic ointment and a sterile bandage.

- Afterward, wash your hands with hot water and soap.

- If the person has not had a recent tetanus shot, suggest they see a doctor.

- You should be extra alert for an infection in a puncture wound because it can spread quickly and make the person very ill. If a puncture wound gets infected, medical attention is needed right away.

CHAPTER 3

Minor Burns

Minor burns and sunburns cause the skin to get red. This kind of burn is called a **first-degree burn**. **Degree** means the amount of burn, how bad it is. A first-degree burn is the least serious kind of burn.

If blisters form on the burn, it is more serious, and is called a **second-degree burn**. Some severe sunburns can be second-degree burns and may not blister.

If blisters form on a burn, do not break them. Breaking a blister turns the burn into an open wound and this makes it easier for germs to get in. If a burn blister breaks, it is a good idea to put antibiotic ointment on the wound before you bandage it to prevent infection. Aloe vera ointment works well on sunburns and other minor burns.

MINOR BURNS

HANDLING MINOR BURNS

Situation:

Person has a first- or second-degree burn.

First Aid:

- If the person has a minor burn, soak it in clean, cold water right away. Keep it soaking for at least 10 minutes.

- Pat dry the burn or blister.

- Put aloe vera ointment on minor burns or sunburns. Put antibiotic ointment on a popped blister.

- Cover the burn or blister with a sterile bandage.

- In the case of a popped blister watch carefully for infection.

- If blisters have formed on a large burn, the person should be checked by a doctor.

CHAPTER 4

Stings and Bites

INSECT STINGS

Most insect stings do not cause more than swelling and pain where the sting happened. In some cases, though, a person could have an allergic reaction to a sting. A person with an allergic reaction might:

- have trouble breathing or swallowing
- feel dizzy or faint
- feel nauseous
- feel very itchy
- have swelling
- get red blotches on their body

These are serious reactions and need fast medical attention. Many people who know they are allergic to bee stings carry a bee-sting kit from their doctor. If this person was stung, you would help them use this kit first, before you did anything else.

STINGS AND BITES

HANDLING INSECT STINGS

Situation:

Person has been stung by an insect (bee, wasp, hornet, ant, etc.)

First Aid:

- If the person has a medical kit for stings, help them use it right away.

- If the stinger is still there, scrape it off or flick it out.

- Wash the affected area with soap and water, if possible.

- If the sting is still hurting, you can make a paste of baking soda and water and put it on the sting area. This can make it less painful.

- Apply ice or a cold compress.

- If the person has trouble breathing or swallowing, is itchy or feels dizzy or faint, get medical help *immediately*.

BITES

Most mouths carry lots of germs, so when a person has been bitten, whether by an animal or a person, you have to be careful to make sure you handle the germs.

- If the nearby skin even *begins* to get puffy or red and looks like an infection may be starting, get medical help.
- If the bite is deep or is a puncture wound, even though it's from a known pet, get medical help right away and don't wait for signs of infection.

Don't take a chance with animal bites.

There is one more important danger to watch out for with animal bites. Sometimes mammals, such as dogs and cats, carry a deadly disease called **rabies** in their **saliva** (the watery liquid in their mouth). They can get it by being bitten by another animal that has it. Dogs and cats sometimes get rabies from wild animals like bats, skunks and raccoons. To help prevent this, dogs and cats can get shots to protect them against rabies.

Rabies can make animals act in odd ways, so if you see a wild animal acting strangely, stay away from it. For example, skunks and raccoons don't usually stay around humans, but if one wanders into a backyard, acting confused and angry, don't go near it.

Bats can also carry rabies, so it is risky to touch a bat, even a dead one. If there is a bat that has gotten inside a building and won't fly out, let an adult know.

If any mammal bites you, it's important to tell your parent or another adult right away.

STINGS AND BITES

If rabies isn't treated, it will kill a person or animal that has it. So, when a person is bitten by an animal, it becomes important to know if the animal has rabies.

If you are bitten by a pet, your doctor and veterinarian can tell you what to do. If it is a wild animal, there is a number to call by looking up "local animal control" for your area. You and an adult should let them know what happened and follow their instructions.

HANDLING BITES

Situation:

A person has been bitten by a mammal (animal or human) and the bite breaks the skin.

First Aid:

- Put on disposable gloves or something else to cover the hands.

- Scrub the bite well with soap and water to remove saliva.

- If the bite is bleeding, put pressure on it using sterile gauze or a clean cloth.

- Apply antibiotic ointment and cover with a bandage.

- Get medical help if:
    - the bite is severe, is a puncture wound, or looks like it may be getting infected.
    - the animal is unfamiliar to you.
    - the animal behaves strangely.
    - the animal that bit you disappears and can't be found.
    - the animal dies.

CHAPTER 5

Something in the Eye

A person's eyes can be easily damaged, so if a person gets something in an eye, deal with it carefully so that the eye isn't scratched or injured further.

When a person gets something in their eye, it can be very uncomfortable. Even a tiny piece of dust or an eyelash can cause a lot of pain.

The person might want to rub their eye to make it feel better. This is not a good idea because it could scratch the eye.

If an object doesn't come out easily, the eye is still painful, or the eye is scratched, leave the eye alone and get medical care right away. Some of the signs of a scratched eye are: feeling like sand is in the eye, pain, continual tears and redness.

Until you see the doctor, keep the eye closed so it does not become more irritated. To do this, cover the closed eye with a gauze pad and tape this in place. This also helps the person remember not to rub it until they see the doctor.

SOMETHING IN THE EYE

HANDLING SOMETHING IN THE EYE

Situation:

Person has something in his or her eye. If eye is scratched.

First Aid:

- The person should first try blinking their eye to get the object to come out naturally.

- With clean hands, pull the person's lower lid down while they look up. Then reverse it, and pull the upper lid up while they look down.

- If that doesn't work, try to wash it out with eye drops, or a medicine dropper filled with clean, warm water. You can also tilt the head back and flush the eye with clean, warm water from a drinking glass.

- If the object doesn't come out easily, the eye is still painful, or the eye is scratched, cover the closed eye with a gauze pad and tape this in place. Then see a doctor.

CHAPTER 6

Skin Poisoning from Plants

In many parts of the country a few plants grow that produce harmful oils in their leaves, stems and roots. Examples of this are poison oak and poison ivy.

When the oils of these plants come in contact with the skin, the skin may become blistered, and itch and swell for days. People call this "getting poison oak (or ivy)" or "having poison oak (or ivy)."

People get poison ivy or poison oak by touching the plant or by touching something else that was in contact with the plant. Sometimes a pet may brush against the plant and then the owner gets it on their hands by petting the animal.

SKIN POISONING FROM PLANTS

HANDLING SKIN POISONING FROM PLANTS

Situation:

Person has brushed against or handled poison ivy or poison oak.

First Aid:

- Thoroughly wash the affected skin with a strong soap and water as soon as possible. This takes the harmful oil off the skin. Dishwashing soap can work well because it is designed to break down grease and oil. There are also products such as Tecnu® or Zanfel® that are good at getting oil from poison ivy or oak off skin and clothing.

- Have the person take off any clothes that came into contact with the plants and carefully turn them inside out to avoid getting more harmful oil on their hands. Then re-wash any skin that touched the clothes, and wash the clothes with laundry soap in a washing machine to get the harmful oil out.

- If the person breaks out in a rash, they should try not to scratch it. To help with the itching, use lotion such as Calamine® lotion.

CHAPTER 7

Sprains

A **sprain** is an injury caused by a joint being twisted or bent in the wrong direction. The joint may swell and become painful for a while. This swelling is caused by extra blood that flows to the area after it is injured. This can make the injury hurt more and heal more slowly.

Usually, the only first aid needed for a sprain is to get the swelling down. This is done by raising the area of the sprain above the level of the heart so less blood can go there, and then cooling the injury with an ice pack or cold, wet towel since this also lessens swelling.

An ice pack can be made by crushing some ice and holding it in a wet towel, or filling a plastic bag with ice water and sealing it. You can even use a bag of frozen vegetables, like peas or corn.

You should never cool an injury with an ice pack for more than 10 or 15 minutes at a time or you can further damage the body part.

You can also wrap the joint with an elastic (Ace®) bandage, if needed. This will help swelling go down and will protect the joint from more injury.

SPRAINS

HANDLING SPRAINS

Situation:

Person has a sprained ankle.

First Aid:

- Rest the ankle by not walking on it.

- Lessen the swelling with an ice pack (limit to 15 minutes) or cold wet towels.

- Wrap with an elastic (Ace®) bandage, if needed. Don't wrap too tightly—you should be able to slip your fingers between the bandage and the person's skin.

- Raise the ankle above the level of the heart to lessen swelling.

- Get medical help if the ankle continues to hurt, or the person can't walk on it. A bone may be broken.

CHAPTER 8

Heat Emergencies

If a person's body becomes overheated (too hot), this can be an emergency that requires first aid. When a body gets heated up, it works to keep itself cool by sweating. Sometimes a person's cooling system can be overworked and their body can lose the ability to cool itself. This causes the person to feel ill and is actually dangerous if not handled.

There are two levels of heat emergencies. They look very different and you should know how to tell them apart.

HEAT EXHAUSTION

Heat exhaustion is a heat emergency where the body's cooling system becomes badly overworked.

What to look for:

- A person with heat exhaustion may feel cool and their skin may feel damp, cool and kind of sticky. They may also be sweating heavily.

- The face can become pale, and they can have cold sweat on their forehead.

HEAT EMERGENCIES

- The person's muscles may cramp up.
- The person may have a headache or be dizzy.
- The person may feel sick to their stomach or throw up.

HEAT STROKE

If the body gets even more overheated, the cooling system can break down completely so the body can no longer cool itself at all. This is called **heat stroke**. It can happen when a person is out in the hot sun for a long time. Doing a lot of exercise or work in hot weather can also cause heat stroke.

A person with heat stroke could die if it is not treated quickly. This is because when a person's body temperature gets very high, the body's organs can stop working. (**Organs** are parts of the body, such as heart, lungs, brain, kidney, etc., that each do specific jobs to keep us healthy and alive.)

What to look for:

Like heat exhaustion

- Breathing is fast and short.
- The person may feel sick to their stomach and throw up.

But with heat stroke

- The person may not just be dizzy or have a headache, they can have a very bad headache, feel so dizzy that they seem confused and anxious, or they may even be unconscious.
- They may become grouchy, and their speech might not be clear.
- The heartbeat is faster than normal.

HEAT EMERGENCIES

- The face becomes red and very hot, and the person may stop sweating even in the heat.

- The body temperature gets very high.

If a person is showing signs of heat stroke, they need medical attention right away.

HEAT EMERGENCIES

HANDLING HEAT EMERGENCIES

Situation:

Person is showing signs of heat exhaustion.

First Aid:

- Move the person to a cool place.

- Have them lie down, and put something under their legs and feet to raise them slightly higher than the body.

- Loosen any clothing. Untie shoes, remove a belt, unfasten any shirt collar. This will help cooling air reach the body.

- Fan the person, and apply cool wet cloths to face, head and neck to cool the body. If you have ice or an ice pack, you could use that to cool them down. You could also put them in a cool shower.

- Give sips of cool water.

Situation:

Person is showing signs of heat stroke.

First Aid:

- Quickly move the person to a cool location. If it is not possible to get indoors, you might get them to an air-conditioned car or even into a shady spot.

- Remove any heavy or excess clothing, such as a sweater or hat.

- Cool the person, especially their head and neck, by spraying cold water, putting them in a cold tub of water, putting on ice packs, or fanning.

- Cover them with dripping wet towels or cloths. Keep the coverings cool by dipping them in cold water or putting cold water on them now and then.

- Give them a cool (not cold) drink.

- Get medical attention fast.

CHAPTER 9

Cold Emergencies

If you go outside in cold weather for very long and are not dressed warmly enough, your body can lose a lot of heat. This can be dangerous to the important organs of your body such as the heart, lungs, liver and kidneys. The area of your body where these organs are located is called your **body core**, because the **core** of something is the center or inside.

In cold weather, your body tries to keep its core warm by keeping more blood in the center of the body. This lessens the blood supply to the hands, feet and outer body parts. When this happens, a person's ears, nose, fingers or feet can become very cold.

FROSTBITE

When a person's toes, fingers, nose or ears become very cold, they can hurt. If they get even colder, they can go numb.

If they continue to get colder still, the blood and tissue can freeze and the skin turn pale. This is called **frostbite**. Usually when this happens, the person is not aware of it because they have lost feeling in that body part.

COLD EMERGENCIES

If these cold body parts are not warmed up soon, they can be seriously damaged.

HYPOTHERMIA

When a person's body continues to lose heat over a long period of time, the blood supply is lessened not only to the hands and feet, but to the rest of the body as well. This includes the brain. This is a dangerous condition called **hypothermia**. *Hypo-* means "below normal" and *thermia* means "temperature or heat."

A person with hypothermia may

- be confused and not able to think clearly. For example, they might try to take off a warm coat because it feels heavy. They might want to lie down and sleep in the cold.
- be clumsy or have trouble walking.
- speak slowly or be hard to understand.
- shiver constantly.

Air temperature does not have to be below freezing for a person to get hypothermia. A lightly dressed person caught in a cold, windy rainstorm or anyone who is not dressed warmly enough for cool weather can lose enough body heat to get hypothermia.

Wind, rain, hunger and exhaustion increase the risk. So, when you are outside in cool or cold weather, you can prevent hypothermia by wearing enough clothing to keep yourself warm and dry, eating plenty of food for energy, and drinking lots of liquids.

COLD EMERGENCIES

The body temperature of a swimmer in cool and cold water drops steadily, so when a swimmer gets cold, they should get out of the water and cover up or exercise to get warm.

Uncontrollable shivering is a sign of the beginning of hypothermia.

COLD EMERGENCIES

HANDLING COLD EMERGENCIES

Situation:

A person's finger or toe is frozen from cold. There is no feeling and there are pale or white patches on the fingers or toes because of the freezing.

First Aid:

- Move the person into a warm place.

- Thaw or warm up the frostbitten body part by putting it in warm, *not hot,* water or against someone's warm body, or by wrapping the body part in a warm blanket or sleeping bag.

- Do not rub or massage frozen skin. That may cause further injury.

- *A person should not walk on feet that have been frostbitten.*

- Get medical attention.

COLD EMERGENCIES

Situation:

A person is showing signs of hypothermia.

First Aid:

- Get the person into a warm place.

- Take off any wet clothes and get the person into warm, dry clothes.

- Put the person under warm covers or into a warm sleeping bag.

- Give the person something warm to drink, if possible.

- If hypothermia is far advanced, the person's body may be too cold to warm up by itself. In this case, use any way you can to *gently* increase the person's body heat.

- If no other source of heat is available, a rescuer can get under the covers with the person to use their own body heat to warm the person suffering from hypothermia. An animal, like a dog, can also be put under the covers to help warm them up.

CHAPTER 10

Choking

Your **windpipe** is the tube that carries air from your nose and mouth to your lungs. The opening to the windpipe is very close to the opening of the tube that carries food to your stomach and sometimes food can get into the windpipe by mistake.

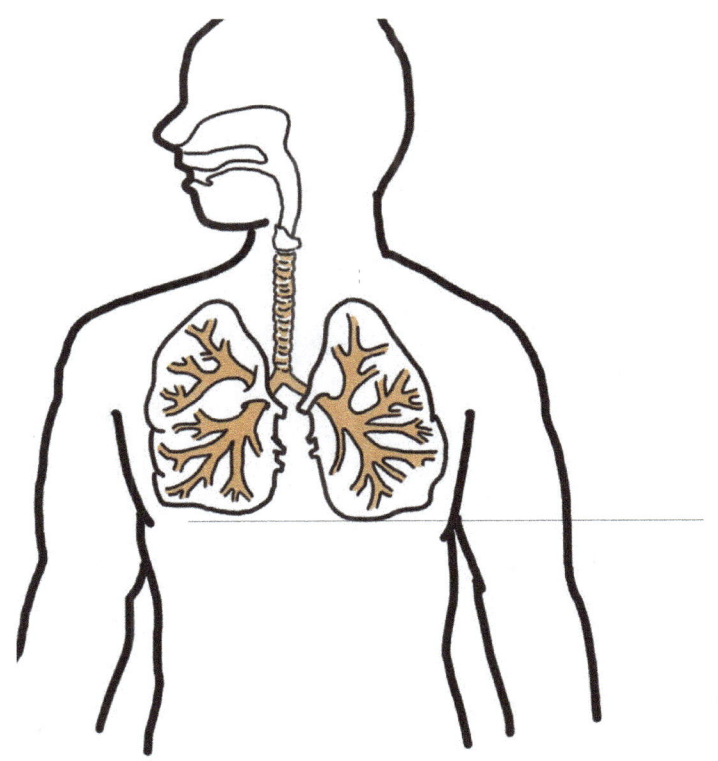

CHOKING

When a person gets food or an object stuck in their windpipe, it makes it difficult or impossible to breathe. The person may choke, cough or be unable to do anything at all. Many people who are choking will put their hands to their throat as a signal that something is wrong.

Before starting first aid, make sure to ask the person if they are choking. If they can breathe or talk, then they might be able to clear their own throat. A person who is truly choking cannot speak or make sounds with their voice.

When you are trying to help a choking person, it is important to let them know what you are doing, and then to act quickly.

HANDLING CHOKING

Situation:

A person is choking and trying to cough.

First Aid:

- Ask the person if they are choking. If they can cough, encourage them to keep coughing until they cough up the thing they are choking on.

- If they can't breathe, cough or talk, get the person to lean forward and hit them five times firmly on the back between the shoulder blades with the heel of your hand, not a fist. These are called **back blows** (a **blow** here means a hit or punch).

    After each back blow, check quickly to see if they are still choking.

- If they are still choking, use **abdominal thrusts**. These are quick pushes on the person's abdomen. Here is how to do an abdominal thrust:

    - Stand behind the person with your arms around their waist.

    - Find the person's rib cage. Clasp your hands together, so that the knuckle of one thumb is above the person's belly button but below their rib cage.

    - With your hands in this position, quickly pull inward and up at the same time. Then relax your arms. This is like squeezing a plastic bottle with a stopper to make the stopper pop out.

CHOKING

- Repeat this five times, checking quickly after each abdominal thrust to see if the person is still choking.

- If the person is still choking after five abdominal thrusts, quickly call 911 or the emergency number for your area.

- Then continue to do five back blows followed by five abdominal thrusts until the thing that is blocking the windpipe pops loose, or help comes.

- As soon as the person can breathe on their own, let go and let them recover. The person should get medical help as soon as possible to be sure they have fully recovered.

CHAPTER 11

Fainting and Blows to the Head

FAINTING

Fainting happens when a person loses consciousness for a while because too little blood is reaching the brain. If a person starts to faint, the main thing to do is get their head below the rest of their body so the blood flows back to the brain. You might be able to keep a person from completely fainting if you do this.

If a person becomes pale and wobbly, have them quickly lie down and put their feet higher than their head. Or they can sit down and put their head between their knees until the feeling passes.

Most people who faint recover quickly if they just lie quietly for a few minutes.

FAINTING AND BLOWS TO THE HEAD

HANDLING FAINTING

Situation:

A person faints and falls to the ground.

First Aid:

- Loosen anything tight around the person's neck or waist and raise their feet about 12 inches above the surface the person is lying on.

- You can put books, folded coats or pillows under the person's feet. The idea is to raise the feet higher than the heart to encourage blood flowing to the brain.

- The person should regain consciousness quickly. Keep the person lying down until fully recovered.

FAINTING AND BLOWS TO THE HEAD

BLOWS TO THE HEAD

A person who has had a blow to the head might feel faint or dizzy. In most cases this feeling goes away in a few minutes, although the person can have pain or a bump where they were hit that lasts for several days.

In some cases, the situation is more serious. Blows to the head can cause a **concussion**, which is an injury to the brain causing it to swell. This might not show up immediately, so you should be alert for any of the signs of concussion as covered below.

The injured person may:

- be unconscious
- start to go unconscious
- have neck pain
- keep feeling faint or dizzy
- be unable to balance
- not be able to speak clearly
- feel confused
- feel sick to their stomach, or throw up

If any of these things happen, the person needs medical help right away.

Do not move a person who has been hit in the head until they are ready to move on their own.

FAINTING AND BLOWS TO THE HEAD

HANDLING A BLOW TO THE HEAD

Situation:

A person has had a blow to the head.

First Aid:

- Help the person lie down, or keep them lying down, until they have fully recovered.

- If they are conscious and seem to be recovering, you can have the person hold an ice pack on the bump. If there is a cut, you can handle this using the first aid steps for a bleeding wound.

- If the person is unconscious or going unconscious, dizzy, feeling sick, throwing up, feeling confused, or in a lot of pain, you should get medical help right away.

- Keep an eye on the person. If any of these things happen *after* they seem to be better, get medical help right away.

CHAPTER 12

Shock

Shock normally means being suddenly surprised by bad news. You would be **shocked** to find out that your bike had been stolen. When the body goes into shock, this is something different. **Shock** is when something like sickness or injury is causing the body to react very badly.

Serious blood loss, **dehydration** (not having enough water) and allergic reactions can all cause the body to go into shock. What is actually happening when the body goes into shock is that the blood is not circulating strongly enough through the body. This can be dangerous.

A person in shock

- feels weak and cold
- may be pale and their skin can feel cold, wet and sort of sticky
- may feel sick to the stomach.

In every accident, the body has some level of shock. It should be watched for and treated as needed.

SHOCK

HANDLING SHOCK

Situation:

A person has been injured and is showing signs of shock.

First Aid:

- Call 911 or the emergency number for your area.

- Have the person lie down with their feet raised about 12 inches above the surface they are lying on. This is to strengthen the blood flow to the brain and important organs.

    If the person has had an injury to their back, neck or head, do not raise their feet because this can cause further injury.

- Cover or wrap the person and keep them warm. Loosen any tight clothing.

- Keep talking with the person calmly and try to help them feel relaxed that help is coming.

- Do not let the person have anything to eat or drink. If they were to become unconscious, they could choke.

CHAPTER 13

Making an Emergency Phone Call

In most situations where first aid is necessary you will be able to handle the situation without emergency help. Even if a person needs to get medical help, he or she can usually get this from their doctor later. However, if you do need to call for emergency help, it is important to know how to do this.

In the U.S. and Canada, the emergency phone number is 911, but it can be different in other countries. When you call this number, you will speak to a dispatcher. This is the person who takes all the information and sends the right kind of help for your situation.

When speaking to the dispatcher, it is important to keep calm and answer all their questions as completely as you can. Things, such as your location, are especially important so they can get help to you quickly.

MAKING AN EMERGENCY PHONE CALL

Do not hang up until the dispatcher tells you it is okay to do so. Sometimes a dispatcher will stay on the phone with you until help arrives. Here are some of the questions you might be asked:

- What's your emergency? (usually asked when the dispatcher answers the call)
- What is your name?
- What is the problem?
- Where did it happen? or What is the address?
- When did it happen? How long ago?
- How many people are hurt?
- What is being done to help them?
- How are they doing?
- What phone number are you calling from?

Answer with complete information and be sure to listen carefully to what the dispatcher tells you.

You may never need to make a 911 call, but it is good to be prepared.

MAKING AN EMERGENCY PHONE CALL

Let's Do This!
PRACTICE EMERGENCY PHONE CALLS

For this activity you will need

- a person to work with

Steps

1. With your partner make up an emergency situation that would require you to call the emergency number for your area.

2. Your partner pretends to be the emergency dispatcher. You pretend to dial 9-1-1 or local emergency number.

3. When you call, your partner reads the script below. You answer all the questions.

4. Do this with different situations until you feel comfortable making an emergency phone call.

Script:

Dispatcher: "(name of town) 9-1-1" (or similar statement). "What's your emergency?"

Student: "There's a fire next door." or "I'm calling to report an accident," etc.

MAKING AN EMERGENCY PHONE CALL

The student then gives the important information clearly enough so the dispatcher can type it into their system.

The dispatcher asks any of the following questions, or similar questions, in any order, to understand exactly what is happening, what kind of help to send and where to send it.

Dispatcher: "What is your name?"

Student replies.

Dispatcher: "What is the problem?"

Student replies.

Dispatcher: "What is the address?" or "Where did it happen?"

Student replies.

Dispatcher: "What phone number are you calling from?"

Student replies.

Dispatcher: "When did it happen?"

Student replies.

Dispatcher: "How many people are hurt?" or "Is he (or she) the only person hurt?" or "How many people are involved?"

Student replies.

Dispatcher: "What help is being given?"

MAKING AN EMERGENCY PHONE CALL

Student replies.

Dispatcher: "Stay on the line. I am going to send help. [pause] Help is on the way."

Depending on the type of problem, the dispatcher might ask other questions and/or give information on how to help the victim until professional help arrives. **Do not hang up until the dispatcher hangs up or tells you to.**

Dispatcher: "You may hang up now."

MAKING AN EMERGENCY PHONE CALL

Let's Do This!
PRACTICE YOUR FIRST AID

For this activity you will need

- objects to use for demonstration
- a partner
- the Drill Sheet for First Aid at the back of the book (p. 91)

Steps

- For each of the situations given, your partner should read you the situation, for example, "**Person has a nosebleed.**"

- You show the first aid steps using objects or by physically demonstrating the actions. Be sure to include making an emergency phone call when appropriate.

- Continue to practice until you feel confident you can correctly show the first aid steps for any situation given.

CHAPTER 14

Emergencies in the Environment

An **emergency** is something that needs attention right away. It could be a sudden flood, a fire or an accident. Since emergencies often happen suddenly and unexpectedly, it is a good idea to have a plan of action for the emergencies that are most likely to happen.

There are things you can learn to prevent emergencies, and to help with emergencies if they do happen. Knowing how to call the emergency services number for your area is part of this.

CHAPTER 15

Electrical Emergencies

Electricity is an important form of energy. It travels through wires and into buildings to help run lights, machines, computers and many things we use every day.

Most electric wires are covered by plastic insulation to keep the electricity safely inside. If this insulation is broken or worn out, electricity can cause injuries.

When a person gets contacted by an amount of electricity that hurts them, whether a little or a lot, we say they received an **electric shock**, which is another definition for the word "shock."

The reason people can receive this kind of shock is because electricity travels very well through water, and a human body is mostly made of water. So, when a person contacts electricity, the electricity runs throughout their body.

ELECTRICAL EMERGENCIES

When a person is receiving a strong electric shock, the electricity can make their muscles stiffen so much that they can't let go of the wire or whatever they grabbed that shocked them. It might seem like a good idea to pull the person away, but this is dangerous. If you touch a person who is being shocked, you could be shocked, too, because the electricity can travel from that person through your body as well.

ELECTRICAL EMERGENCIES

HANDLING ELECTRICAL EMERGENCIES

Indoor Wires

If a person is being shocked, the first thing to do is turn off the electricity. If you can reach the plug safely, pull it out. Sometimes just turning off the wall switch will turn off the electricity.

You can also turn off the circuit breaker. (Wires in a house make a path for electricity to follow--called a **circuit**. The **circuit breaker** is a switch that breaks the path and turns off electricity to a whole room or part of a house. Switches for all the circuits in a house can be found in the **circuit box**. It's a good idea to know where this is.)

Situation:

A person is being shocked by a worn or broken electrical cord, and can't let go.

Actions:

- Don't touch the person.

- Turn off the electricity.

    o If you can get to the wall socket safely and the cord is not broken or wet, pull the plug from the socket.

    or

    o Turn off the power with the wall switch.

    or

    o If these don't work, turn off the main power at the circuit breaker, if possible.

ELECTRICAL EMERGENCIES

- Give first aid if the person has been burned.

- If the person has been badly shocked, call 911 (or the emergency number for your area).

ELECTRICAL EMERGENCIES

Outdoor Wires

The thick electric wires attached to telephone poles are called **power lines**. These bring electricity to all the buildings in a neighborhood, so they carry much more electricity than house wires. In a storm they can be torn down by wind or falling branches, and hang low or lie on the ground.

A power line that has electricity traveling through it is called a **live wire**. Sometimes there are sparks, smoke and fire where a live power line is touching the ground. But a power line can still be live even when you don't see these.

Getting close to one of these power lines can give a bad shock, so stay far away (at least 50 feet, but more is better).

If you happen to be closer than 50 feet, shuffle away, being careful not to lift your feet as doing this can cause you to be shocked.

Situation:

Low-hanging or fallen power line outdoors.

Actions:

- Don't touch the power line or anything in contact with it, even a person.

- Stay as far away as possible (more than 50 feet).

- If you are closer than 50 feet, shuffle away from the power line, being careful not to lift your feet.

- Call 911 or your emergency number and report the location of the power line.

CHAPTER 16

Fire Emergencies

Fires are not common, but they do happen. There are things that you and your family can do to lessen the chance that you will be hurt by one.

Using candles safely, keeping a fire extinguisher handy in the kitchen or near a fireplace, and keeping matches stored where small children cannot find them—these all help prevent fires in the first place.

Having working smoke detectors in your home makes it more likely that you would get warning of a fire, and would be able to get out of the house quickly if you needed to.

FIRE EMERGENCIES

HOW TO PUT OUT SMALL FIRES

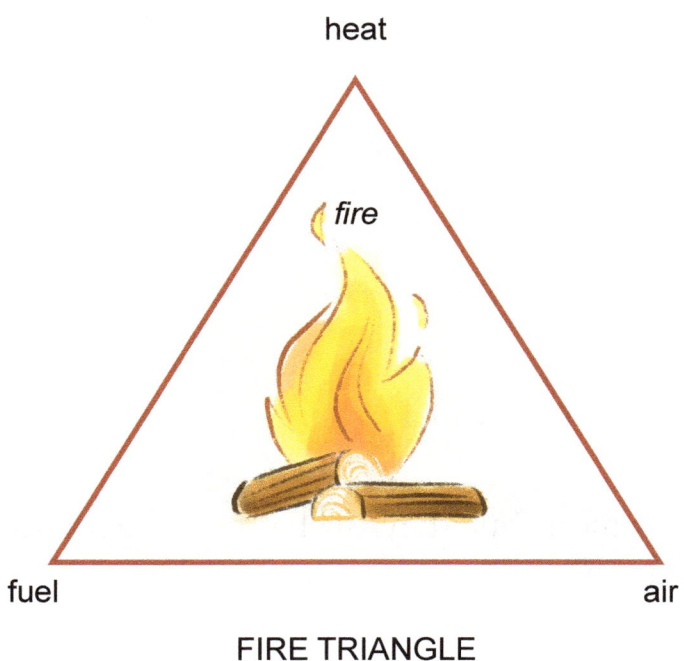

FIRE TRIANGLE

When you understand how a fire burns, it is easier to put it out. Fires need three things to burn: fuel, heat and air. If you take away one or more of these, the fire goes out. How you do this depends on what is burning, and what you have nearby that you can use.

Fuel. This is what is on fire, like wood or paper. If all the fuel has burned up, a fire will go out. You can sometimes move burning material to a place where it will not spread, and then it can burn out safely. For example, you might carry a small trash can outdoors or move a pan off a hot stove.

You can also move burnable things away from a fire. For example, you could clear away wood or paper near a campfire. The fire won't spread if it has nothing new to burn.

FIRE EMERGENCIES

Heat. When things burn, they get hot. The heat then keeps the fire going. By cooling the thing that is burning (whatever the fire is using for fuel), you can put out a fire. This is why firefighters pour water on a fire; it cools the burning material and puts it out. Here are some things you could use to cool a fire:

- water
- snow
- wet leaves
- wet dirt or sand
- a wet blanket or towel

However, *don't* use water or wet cloth on electrical or oil fires. When you use water on an electrical fire, you can be shocked. When you put water on an oil fire, the oil may spatter and spread the fire.

Air. A fire needs air to burn. If there is no more air, the fire will go out. Here are some ways to cut off air to a fire:

- Cover it with a wet blanket or towel.
- Cover it with dirt or sand—it doesn't even need to be wet.
- If the fire is in a pan or a trash can, cover it with a lid.
- If the fire is in a pan, you can pour on enough salt or baking soda to cover the fire and put it out. These are used because they will not catch fire.

FIRE EMERGENCIES

USING FIRE EXTINGUISHERS

When you **extinguish** a flame or fire, you make it stop burning. A **fire extinguisher** is a metal container filled with a powdery chemical that can put out small fires. It does this both by cooling the fire and keeping fresh air out of it.

There are different types of fires, and fire extinguishers are labeled according to the type of fire they can put out:

- Type A is used on things that burn easily, like paper, wood, cloth and plastics.

- Type B is used on burning liquids like gasoline, kerosene, grease and oil.

- Type C is used on electrical fires.

Most fire extinguishers you will see are marked "ABC" and can be used on all three types. Here is a fire extinguisher with the main parts labeled.

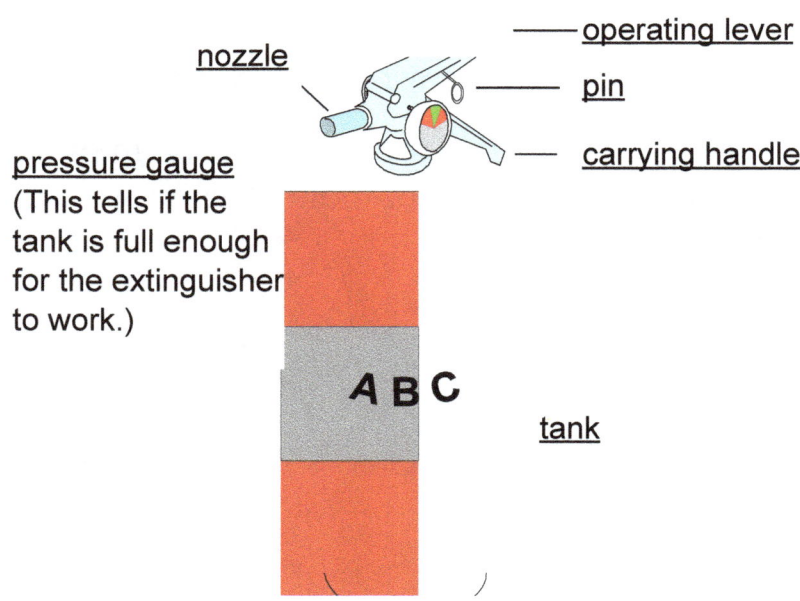

FIRE EMERGENCIES

Here is how to use a common ABC fire extinguisher:

1. Hold the fire extinguisher in your hands or hold it by the carrying handle.

2. Set it down on a solid surface.

3. Pull out the pin in the operating lever. This unlocks it so you will be able to squeeze together the operating lever and carrying handle.

4. Hold the fire extinguisher by the carrying handle and carry it to the fire.

5. Stand about six feet back from the fire, and aim the nozzle at the bottom of the fire.

6. Squeeze the operating lever and carrying handle together and spray in short bursts. If the spray misses, adjust your distance from the fire.

FIRE EMERGENCIES

7. Spray from side to side until the fire is out.

FIRE EMERGENCY PLAN

It is a good idea to have a family escape plan in case a larger fire happens in your house. The plan should include:

- Two ways (if possible) to get out of every room or area in your home.
- A safe place outside where all family members can meet when they get out of the house. This way you know everyone is out.

Your family should drill the plan. This is like doing a fire drill at school.

You could start with each person in their bedroom. Have one person press the alarm button on a smoke detector to start the drill. This lets you hear the sound you will need to recognize in a real fire. Everyone should get out of the house using the plan and go to the outside meeting place.

You could also practice with people in other rooms besides their bedrooms. The idea is to know the plan well so you remember it in an emergency.

Even a little fire can make a lot of smoke and make it hard to see or breathe. Because smoke rises, the air can be clearer near the floor, so if you crawl close to the floor to exit, you will be able to breathe better.

When you are making your fire plan, it might be a good idea to think about how you would get out of your house if you had to crawl through smoke. You might even want to practice this.

FIRE EMERGENCIES

HANDLING FIRE EMERGENCIES

Small Fires

Situation:

Paper fire in a trash can.

Action:

- If you can handle it safely, take the trash can outside to burn out.

    or

- Smother the fire with wet towels, a lid, or a fire extinguisher.

FIRE EMERGENCIES

Situation:

Oil fire in a frying pan.

Oil burns easily, and burning oil can splash out of a pan and spread a fire. It can also cause burns.

When you are handling a pan with burning oil, move it gently. Don't put the pan under running water, or add water to it, because this can make hot oil spatter and cause burns.

Action:

- Smother the fire. You could cover the pan with a lid or pour on salt or baking soda.

    or

- Carefully remove the pan from the burner and let the fire burn out. Just set it aside. Do not run outside with the pan because that might splash burning oil around.

FIRE EMERGENCIES

Situation:

Clothes on fire.

If a person's clothes are on fire, the thing to remember is "**Stop, drop and roll.**" Running or waving arms only gives the fire more air and makes it burn more. The person should drop to the ground, and roll back and forth to cut off air to the fire.

Actions:

- **Stop.** Don't run.

- **Drop** to the ground and cover face with hands.

- **Roll** back and forth to smother the flames.

- Call 911 or your emergency number if there is still a fire or if the person is badly burned. (Always make sure burning clothes are out before doing anything else.)

FIRE EMERGENCIES

Situation:

Electrical fire indoors.

A worn or broken wire can start a fire if it touches wood or some other material that can burn.

Actions:

- Turn off the power.

- Put out the fire with an ABC (or BC) fire extinguisher. Do not use water because you might get shocked.

- If you can't turn off the power, you can still try to put out the fire with the fire extinguisher if you can get to it safely.

BUILDING ON FIRE

If you see a burning building, call for emergency assistance right away. Then you can shout or make noise to get people to come out. If you try to go into a burning building to help other people, you can get hurt.

Here are some points to remember if you have to get out of a burning building:

- Try to get out quickly.

- If you have to open a door, check it for heat and smoke first. If the door feels hot or smoke is coming in, don't open it as this could give the fire more air. Get out another way.

- If the door is cool and no smoke is coming in, open it slowly. If it turns out there is smoke or fire on the other side of the door, shut it quickly and find another way out.

- Use stairs not elevators because an elevator shaft acts like a chimney for fire and smoke. Also, the elevator might not work if the electricity goes off.

- Try to avoid inhaling smoke. Stay low, and cover your mouth and nose with a cloth or even your shirt or jacket. A saying to remember is, "**Stay low and go**."

FIRE EMERGENCIES

Situation:

You notice a building on fire.

Actions:

- Call 911 or your emergency number.

- Get the people to come out by shouting to them or banging on the door.

- Offer your help to people who come out.

FIRE EMERGENCIES

Situation:

You are inside a building on fire.

Actions:

- Try to get out quickly.

- If you have to open a door, check it for heat and smoke first.

- If the door feels hot or smoke is coming in, don't open it. Get out another way.

- If the door is cool and no smoke is coming in, open it slowly to check for smoke or fire. If it turns out there is smoke or fire, shut it quickly and find another way out.

- Stay low to the floor for fresher air. Cover your mouth with a cloth or even your shirt or jacket.

FIRE EMERGENCIES

- Use stairs to get out of a burning building, not elevators.

- If there is an outside meeting place, go there quickly.

- Call 911 or your emergency number for help.

CHAPTER 17

Water Emergencies

A person who is in trouble in the water, but not actually drowning, is able to kick, wave their arms and shout for help. This could be called "near-drowning." The person needs help getting out of the water right away, because if they are not helped, they can begin to actually drown.

A person who is drowning does not look like you might expect from movies or TV shows. They can't call for help because they are just trying to breathe. Their head is usually not very high out of the water. They might go under the water and then come back up—but not far. The person's arms may be out to their sides pushing on the water; they may even look like they are trying to climb an invisible ladder.

If you are not sure what is happening, you can call to the person and ask if they are okay. If they don't answer, it is likely because they are drowning and can't. They need immediate help.

Unless you are a trained lifeguard and know how to handle a drowning person in the water, do not try to swim to help the person. You could be pulled under and get into trouble yourself. (Of course, if it is a small child who is having trouble in the water, you could go to them as long as you can keep your feet on the bottom of the pool or ground and stay balanced.)

When a person is in trouble in the water, the thing to remember is "**Call, reach, throw, go.**"

HANDLING WATER EMERGENCIES

Situation:

Person in trouble in the water or drowning.

Actions:

- **Call for help.** Tell the lifeguard if there is one. Have someone call 911 or the local emergency number because medical help will be needed after the person is out of the water.

- **Reach**. Try to reach the person with your hand or foot.

    If you are on the side of a pool or on a dock, lie down flat first. This is so you don't get pulled in when the person grabs onto you.

    If you are in the water, hold on to something solid like the pool ladder or the edge of a dock, and then reach for the person.

    You can also reach with a strong pole or a broom.

- **Throw** the person something that will float, like a lifeguard ring, a lifejacket or even a foam cooler. It is best to throw something that has a rope attached that you can pull on after the person is hanging on.

- **Go.** You could go to the person with a boat or surfboard if that was the only way to help.

- Get medical help for the person right away, even if it looks like they have recovered.

WATER EMERGENCIES

Situation:

Person has fallen through ice into freezing water.

Ice that is not fully frozen can crack and a person walking on it can end up in the water. Walking over the ice to help a person who has fallen in can be dangerous since the ice could break under you, too.

Actions:

- Try to reach the person from shore or give them something to grab onto from the shore, such as a stick, broom or rope. (You can tie something to the end of the rope and throw it to the person.)

- If that doesn't work, lie down on the ice to reach the person. This spreads your weight so the ice is less likely to crack under you.

- Once the person is holding on, you can pull them out. If you are grasping them directly, hold onto them by the wrists to pull them out.

- After you pull the person out of the water, get them out of wet clothing, dried off and warmed up.

CHAPTER 18

Emergencies in Nature

Some common emergencies in nature are tornados, earthquakes, floods and thunderstorms. Floods and storms are not always emergencies, but can be if they are sudden or you are not prepared.

In each of these situations the important thing is to get into a position of safety until the danger is over. If any of these emergencies are common in your area, it's a good idea to have a plan in mind before they happen since you will probably need to act quickly.

EMERGENCIES IN NATURE

TORNADOS

If you are indoors:

- Go to a **storm shelter**. This is a sturdy underground room used for protection from a storm.

- If you can't get to a storm shelter, try to get into a basement.

- If this is not possible, get into a room or closet on the lowest floor close to the center of a building (called the interior of the building).

- Stay away from windows because glass could break and fly around.

- If possible, get under a heavy table.

- Cover your body with a blanket, coat or some other thick cloth to protect you from flying glass, and be sure to protect your head.

If you are outdoors:

- Lie down on the ground in the lowest place you can find. This way you are less likely to be hit by flying objects.

- Cover your head and face with your arms.

- Do not hide under a bridge or overpass because the wind of the tornado is stronger in those places.

EMERGENCIES IN NATURE

HANDLING TORNADO EMERGENCIES

Situation:

You are indoors and a tornado is coming.

Actions:

- Go to a storm cellar, a basement or an interior room on the lowest floor.

- Stay away from windows.

- If possible, get under a heavy table.

- Cover your body with a blanket, coat or some other thick cloth to protect you from flying glass and be sure to protect your head.

EMERGENCIES IN NATURE

Situation:

You are outdoors and a tornado is coming.

Actions:

- Lie down on the ground in the lowest place you can find.

- Cover your head and face with your arms.

- Do not hide under a bridge or overpass because the wind of the tornado is stronger in those places.

- Stay there until the tornado is over.

EMERGENCIES IN NATURE

EARTHQUAKES

In an earthquake, buildings can shake and objects can fall down. It can be impossible to walk because the ground is shaking so hard.

If you are inside a building when an earthquake begins:

- The best choice is to get under something strong like a table or desk so you will be safe from things that fall down.

    Crouch down and hold on to the leg of the table or desk. This will help you stay under the shelter.

- Keep away from windows because glass can shatter and be thrown around.

- Taking shelter in a basement is not a good idea in an earthquake, since part of the house could fall into the basement.

If you are outdoors, move away from any buildings, electric power lines or other things that can fall. Crouch down and cover your head with your arms.

If you are in a car, pull over and stop driving—but don't park on or under a bridge or overpass, as these can collapse. Stay in the car until the earthquake stops.

EMERGENCIES IN NATURE

HANDLING EARTHQUAKE EMERGENCIES

Situation:

An earthquake starts when you are indoors.

Actions:

- Stay away from windows.

- Get under a solid piece of furniture.

- Hang on so you don't get thrown from cover.

- Protect your head.

EMERGENCIES IN NATURE

Situation

An earthquake starts when you are outdoors.

Actions:

- Get as far away as you can from buildings, power lines or other things that can fall on you.

- Crouch down and cover your head.

EMERGENCIES IN NATURE

Situation

An earthquake starts when you are in a car.

Actions:

- Pull over and stop driving—but don't park on or under a bridge or overpass, as these can collapse.

- Stay in the car until the earthquake stops.

EMERGENCIES IN NATURE

FLOODS

Floods can happen after heavy rain storms, and the rushing water can be dangerous. The best thing to do in a flood is get to a higher position. You can climb a tree, go up a hill, or go to the higher floors of a building. Avoid walking through fast-moving water because it can knock you down.

If you are caught in a flood while in a car, do not try to drive through it. This is because rushing flood water can carry away a car. If you can, get out of the car and go to a higher position, trying not to walk through moving water.

HANDLING FLOOD EMERGENCIES

Situation:

Sudden flood

Actions:

- Get to higher ground without walking through moving water.

- If in a car and you can do it safely, leave the car and get to higher ground without walking through moving water.

EMERGENCIES IN NATURE

THUNDERSTORMS

Lightning is a very powerful, hot burst of electrical energy. When this electricity travels through air, it causes tiny air parts to vibrate and collide, making thunder. Even if you can't see lightning, thunder lets you know it is happening.

Since lightning is so hot, it is dangerous to be near where it strikes. Lightning is usually drawn to whatever is sticking up highest in an area. This could be a tall tree, a metal tower or a person standing in a flat field. That is why you may have heard you should not stand under a tree in a thunderstorm. Lightning is so powerful that if it were to strike the tree, you could be hurt.

If you are outdoors when a thunderstorm starts, there are some things you can do to keep yourself safe.

- You can get into a car or building.

- If you are not close to cars and buildings, get away from high points, such as the top of a hill or a tree standing alone, and move to a low point.

- In the woods, go into an area with lots of low trees and away from tall ones.

- Crouch down like a ball with your head tucked in so you are as small and low as possible but touching the ground as little as possible.

- Never lie down on the ground, even if you are in an open space, as that makes you a bigger target for lightning.

EMERGENCIES IN NATURE

HANDLING THUNDERSTORM EMERGENCIES

Situation:

A thunderstorm starts near you.

Actions:

- If you can get to a building, go indoors, or get into a car.

- If you are in a car, stay there.

- If you are outdoors, move to the lowest point you can find.

- Crouch down and make yourself as small and low as possible, but touching the ground as little as possible. Don't lie down.

Let's Do This!
PRACTICE HANDLING EMERGENCIES IN THE ENVIRONMENT

For this activity you will need

- objects to use for demonstration
- a partner
- the Drill Sheet for Handling Emergencies in the Environment at the back of the book (p. 111)

Steps

- For each of the situations given, your partner should read you the situation, for example, "**There is a paper fire in a trashcan.**"

- You show the actions to take using objects or by physically demonstrating the actions. Be sure to include making an emergency phone call when appropriate.

- Continue to practice until you feel confident you can correctly show the actions to take for any situation given.

Drill Sheet for First Aid

WOUNDS AND BLEEDING

Special Note on Bleeding
Be careful not to get another person's blood on your own hands, because you can get a disease more easily that way. If available, wear disposable gloves. If gloves are not available, place some other barrier between the blood and your hands. A clean plastic bag might work well. And *always* wash your own hands well after you give first aid to someone who is bleeding, even if you wear gloves.

Situation:

Person has a small wound or scratch with little bleeding.

First Aid:

- Put on disposable gloves or something else as a barrier.

- Clean out of the wound anything you can see, such as dirt, gravel or other things. Rinse the wound with water, and wash around it with soap and water. Let the skin dry.

- If you have antibiotic ointment, put it on the wound.

- Put on a sterile bandage. If you do not have a bandage and the wound is small, you could leave it uncovered.

- Afterward, wash your hands well with hot water and soap.

- If the wound was dirty, have the injured person watch out for infection, and get medical attention if needed.

DRILL SHEET FOR FIRST AID

Situation:

Person has a wound or cut, and the bleeding does not stop right away.

First Aid:

- Put on disposable gloves or something else to cover your hands.

- Cover the wound with a sterile bandage, or a clean pad or cloth if a bandage isn't available.

- Have the injured person press hard enough to stop the blood flow, or if they can't, do it yourself.

- If the wound is on an arm or leg and the bleeding doesn't stop quickly, raise the arm or leg above the level of the heart. This will help stop the bleeding faster.

- After the bleeding has stopped, put on a new sterile bandage.

- Afterward, wash your hands well with hot water and soap.

- If it's a larger wound, have the injured person get immediate medical attention.

DRILL SHEET FOR FIRST AID

Situation:

Person has a nosebleed.

First Aid:

- Put on disposable gloves or something else to cover your hands.

- Have the person sit up, lean forward, breathe through their mouth, and pinch the soft part of their nostrils together (just below the bone) for ten minutes. You can also hold a cold, wet cloth to their nose and face while they are pinching.

- If the bleeding doesn't stop after 10 minutes, pinch it for another 10 minutes.

- The person should not blow their nose for several hours after the bleeding stops.

- Afterward, wash your hands well with hot water and soap.

DRILL SHEET FOR FIRST AID

Situation:

Person has a puncture wound with little bleeding (for example, stepped on a nail or a large splinter).

First Aid:

- Put on disposable gloves or something else as a barrier.

- Clean out of the wound anything you can see, such as dirt, gravel or other things. Then gently press around the wound to help it bleed. Getting any blood or pus out of the wound may help clean it.

- Wash the wound well with soap and water.

- Put on antibiotic ointment and a sterile bandage.

- Afterward, wash your hands with hot water and soap.

- If the person has not had a recent tetanus shot, suggest they see a doctor.

- You should be extra alert for an infection in a puncture wound because it can spread quickly and make the person very ill. If a puncture wound gets infected, medical attention is needed right away.

DRILL SHEET FOR FIRST AID

MINOR BURNS

Situation:

Person has a first- or second-degree burn.

First Aid:

- If the person has a minor burn, soak it in clean, cold water right away. Keep it soaking for at least 10 minutes.

- Pat dry the burn or blister.

- Put aloe vera ointment on minor burns or sunburns. Put antibiotic ointment on a popped blister.

- Cover the burn or blister with a sterile bandage.

- In the case of a popped blister watch carefully for infection.

- If blisters have formed on a large burn, the person should be checked by a doctor.

DRILL SHEET FOR FIRST AID

INSECT STINGS AND BITES

Situation:

Person has been stung by an insect (bee, wasp, hornet, ant, etc.)

First Aid:

- If the person has a medical kit for stings, help them use it right away.

- If the stinger is still there, scrape it off or flick it out.

- Wash the affected area with soap and water, if possible.

- Optional: Make a paste of baking soda and water and put it on the sting area. This can make it less painful.

- Apply ice or a cold compress.

- If the person has trouble breathing or swallowing, is itchy or feels dizzy or faint, get medical help *immediately*.

DRILL SHEET FOR FIRST AID

Situation:

A person has been bitten by a mammal (animal or human) and the bite breaks the skin.

First Aid:

- Put on disposable gloves or something else to cover the hands.

- Scrub the bite well with soap and water to remove saliva.

- If the bite is bleeding, put pressure on it using sterile gauze or a clean cloth.

- Apply antibiotic ointment and cover with a bandage.

- Get medical help if:

    - the bite is severe, is a puncture wound, or looks like it may be getting infected.
    - the animal is unfamiliar to you.
    - the animal behaves strangely.
    - the animal that bit you disappears and can't be found.
    - the animal dies.

DRILL SHEET FOR FIRST AID

SOMETHING IN THE EYE

Situation:

Person has something in his or her eye. If eye is scratched.

First Aid:

- The person should first try blinking their eye to get the object to come out naturally.

- With clean hands, pull the person's lower lid down while they look up. Then reverse it, and pull the upper lid up while they look down.

- If that doesn't work, try to wash it out with eye drops, or a medicine dropper filled with clean, warm water. You can also tilt the head back and flush the eye with clean, warm water from a drinking glass.

- If the object doesn't come out easily, the eye is still painful, or the eye is scratched, cover the closed eye with a gauze pad and tape this in place. Then see a doctor.

SKIN POISONING FROM PLANTS

Situation:

Person has brushed against or handled poison ivy or poison oak.

First Aid:

- Thoroughly wash the affected skin with a strong soap and water as soon as possible. This takes the harmful oil off the skin. Dishwashing soap can work well because it is designed to break down grease and oil. There are also products such as Tecnu® or Zanfel® that are good at getting oil from poison ivy or oak off skin and clothing.

- Have the person take off any clothes that came into contact with the plants and carefully turn them inside out to avoid getting more harmful oil on their hands. Then re-wash any skin that touched the clothes, and wash the clothes with laundry soap in a washing machine to get the harmful oil out.

- If the person breaks out in a rash, they should try not to scratch it. To help with the itching, use lotion such as Calamine® lotion.

DRILL SHEET FOR FIRST AID

SPRAINS

Situation:

Person has a sprained ankle.

First Aid:

- Rest the ankle by not walking on it.

- Lessen the swelling with an ice pack (limit to 15 minutes) or cold wet towels.

- Wrap with an elastic (Ace®) bandage, if needed. Don't wrap too tightly—you should be able to slip your fingers between the bandage and the person's skin.

- Raise the ankle above the level of the heart to lessen swelling.

- Get medical help if the ankle continues to hurt, or the person can't walk on it. A bone may be broken.

DRILL SHEET FOR FIRST AID

HEAT EMERGENCIES

Situation:

Person is showing signs of heat exhaustion.

First Aid:

- Move the person to a cool place.

- Have them lie down, and put something under their legs and feet to raise them slightly higher than the body.

- Loosen any clothing. Untie shoes, remove a belt, unfasten any shirt collar. This will help cooling air reach the body.

- Fan the person, and apply cool wet cloths to face, head and neck to cool the body. If you have ice or an ice pack, you could use that to cool them down. You could also put them in a cool shower.

- Give sips of cool water.

DRILL SHEET FOR FIRST AID

Situation:

Person is showing signs of heat stroke.

First Aid:

- Quickly move the person to a cool location. If it is not possible to get indoors, you might get them to an air-conditioned car or even into a shady spot.

- Remove any heavy or excess clothing, such as a sweater or hat.

- Cool the person, especially their head and neck, by spraying cold water, putting them in a cold tub of water, putting on ice packs, or fanning.

- Cover them with dripping wet towels or cloths. Keep the coverings cool by dipping them in cold water or putting cold water on them now and then.

- Give them a cool (not cold) drink.

- Get medical attention fast.

COLD EMERGENCIES

Situation:

A person's finger or toe is frozen from cold. There is no feeling and there are pale or white patches on the fingers or toes because of the freezing.

First Aid:

- Move the person into a warm place.

- Thaw or warm up the frostbitten body part by putting it in warm, *not hot,* water or against someone's warm body, or by wrapping the body part in a warm blanket or sleeping bag.

  Do not rub or massage frozen skin. That may cause further injury.

  A person should not walk on feet that have been frostbitten.

- Get medical attention.

DRILL SHEET FOR FIRST AID

Situation:

A person is showing signs of hypothermia.

First Aid:

- Get the person into a warm place.

- Take off any wet clothes and get the person into warm, dry clothes.

- Put the person under warm covers or into a warm sleeping bag.

- Give the person something warm to drink, if possible.

- If hypothermia is far advanced, the person's body may be too cold to warm up by itself. In this case, use any way you can to *gently* increase the person's body heat.

- If no other source of heat is available, a rescuer can get under the covers with the person to use their own body heat to warm the person suffering from hypothermia. An animal, like a dog, can also be put under the covers to help warm them up.

DRILL SHEET FOR FIRST AID

CHOKING

Situation:

A person is choking and trying to cough.

First Aid:

- Ask the person if they are choking. If they can cough, encourage them to keep coughing until they cough up the thing they are choking on.

- If they can't breathe, cough or talk, get the person to lean forward and hit them five times firmly on the back between the shoulder blades with the heel of your hand, not a fist. These are called back blows (a blow here means a hit or punch).

   After each back blow, check quickly to see if they are still choking.

- If they are still choking, use abdominal thrusts. These are quick pushes on the person's abdomen. Here is how to do an abdominal thrust:

   - Stand behind the person with your arms around their waist.

   - Find the person's rib cage. Clasp your hands together, so that the knuckle of one thumb is above the person's belly button but below their rib cage.

   - With your hands in this position, quickly pull inward and up at the same time. Then relax your arms. This is like squeezing a plastic bottle with a stopper to make the stopper pop out.

- o Repeat this five times, checking quickly after each abdominal thrust to see if the person is still choking.

- If the person is still choking after five abdominal thrusts, quickly call 911 or the emergency number for your area.

- Then continue to do five back blows followed by five abdominal thrusts until the thing that is blocking the windpipe pops loose, or help comes.

- As soon as the person can breathe on their own, let go and let them recover. The person should get medical help as soon as possible to be sure they have fully recovered.

DRILL SHEET FOR FIRST AID

FAINTING, BLOW TO THE HEAD

Situation:

A person faints and falls to the ground.

First Aid:

- Loosen anything tight around the person's neck or waist and raise their feet about 12 inches above the surface the person is lying on.

    You can put books, folded coats or pillows under the person's feet. The idea is to raise the feet higher than the heart to encourage blood flowing to the brain.

- The person should regain consciousness quickly. Keep the person lying down until fully recovered.

DRILL SHEET FOR FIRST AID

Situation:

A person has had a blow to the head.

First Aid:

- Help the person lie down, or keep them lying down, until they have fully recovered.

- If they are conscious and seem to be recovering, you can have the person hold an ice pack on the bump. If there is a cut, you can handle this using the first aid steps for a bleeding wound.

- If the person is unconscious or going unconscious, dizzy, feeling sick, throwing up, feeling confused, or in a lot of pain, you should get medical help right away.

- Keep an eye on the person. If any of these things happen after they seem to be better, get medical help right away.

DRILL SHEET FOR FIRST AID

SHOCK

Situation:

A person has been injured and is showing signs of shock.

First Aid:

- Call 911 or the emergency number for your area.

- Have the person lie down with their feet raised about 12 inches above the surface they are lying on. This is to strengthen the blood flow to the brain and important organs.

  If the person has had an injury to their back, neck or head, do not raise their feet because this can cause further injury.

- Cover or wrap the person and keep them warm. Loosen any tight clothing.

- Keep talking with the person calmly and try to help them feel relaxed that help is coming.

- Do not let the person have anything to eat or drink. If they were to become unconscious, they could choke.

Drill Sheet for Handling Emergencies in the Environment

ELECTRICAL EMERGENCIES

Indoor Wires

Situation:

A person is being shocked by a worn or broken electrical cord, and can't let go.

Actions:

- Don't touch the person.
- Turn off the electricity.
  - If you can get to the wall socket safely and the cord is not broken or wet, pull the plug from the socket.

    or

  - Turn off the power with the wall switch.

    or

  - If these don't work, turn off the main power at the circuit breaker, if possible.
- Give first aid if the person has been burned.
- If the person has been badly shocked, call 911 (or the emergency number for your area).

DRILL SHEET FOR HANDLING EMERGENCIES IN THE ENVIRONMENT

Outdoor Wires

Situation:

Low-hanging or fallen power line outdoors.

Actions:

- Don't touch the power line or anything in contact with it, even a person.

- Stay as far away as possible (more than 50 feet).

- If you are closer than 50 feet, shuffle away from the power line, being careful not to lift your feet.

- Call 911 or your emergency number and report the location of the power line.

DRILL SHEET FOR HANDLING EMERGENCIES IN THE ENVIRONMENT

FIRE EMERGENCIES

Small Fires

Situation:

Paper fire in a trash can.

Action:

- If you can handle it safely, take the trash can outside to burn out.

    or

- Smother the fire with wet towels, a lid, or a fire extinguisher.

DRILL SHEET FOR HANDLING EMERGENCIES IN THE ENVIRONMENT

Situation:

Oil fire in a frying pan.

Oil burns easily, and burning oil can splash out of a pan and spread a fire. It can also cause burns.

When you are handling a pan with burning oil, move it gently. Don't put the pan under running water, or add water to it, because this can make hot oil spatter and cause burns.

Action:

- Smother the fire. You could cover the pan with a lid or pour on salt or baking soda.

    or

- Carefully remove the pan from the burner and let the fire burn out. Just set it aside. Do not run outside with the pan because that might splash burning oil around.

DRILL SHEET FOR HANDLING EMERGENCIES IN THE ENVIRONMENT

Situation:

Clothes on fire.

Actions:

- **Stop**. Don't run.

- **Drop** to the ground and cover face with hands.

- **Roll** back and forth to smother the flames.

- Call 911 or your emergency number if there is still a fire or if the person is badly burned. (Always make sure burning clothes are out before doing anything else.)

DRILL SHEET FOR HANDLING EMERGENCIES IN THE ENVIRONMENT

BUILDING ON FIRE

Situation:

You notice a building on fire.

Actions:

- Call 911 or your emergency number.

- Get the people to come out by shouting to them or banging on the door.

- Offer your help to people who come out.

DRILL SHEET FOR HANDLING EMERGENCIES IN THE ENVIRONMENT

Situation:

You are inside a building on fire.

Actions:

- Try to get out quickly.

- If you have to open a door, check it for heat and smoke first.

- If the door feels hot or smoke is coming in, don't open it. Get out another way.

- If the door is cool and no smoke is coming in, open it slowly to check for smoke or fire. If it turns out there is smoke or fire, shut it quickly and find another way out.

- Stay low to the floor for fresher air. Cover your mouth with a cloth or even your shirt or jacket.

- Use stairs to get out of a burning building, not elevators.

- If there is an outside meeting place, go there quickly.

- Call 911 or your emergency number for help.

DRILL SHEET FOR HANDLING EMERGENCIES IN THE ENVIRONMENT

WATER EMERGENCIES

Situation:

Person in trouble in the water or drowning.

Actions:

- **Call for help**. Tell the lifeguard if there is one. Have someone call 911 or the local emergency number because medical help will be needed after the person is out of the water.

- **Reach**. Try to reach the person with your hand or foot.

    If you are on the side of a pool or on a dock, lie down flat first. This is so you don't get pulled in when the person grabs onto you.

    If you are in the water, hold on to something solid like the pool ladder or the edge of a dock, and then reach for the person.

    You can also reach with a strong pole or a broom.

- **Throw** the person something that will float, like a lifeguard ring, a lifejacket or even a foam cooler. It is best to throw something that has a rope attached that you can pull on after the person is hanging on.

- **Go**. You could go to the person with a boat or surfboard if that was the only way to help.

- Get medical help for the person right away, even if it looks like they have recovered.

DRILL SHEET FOR HANDLING EMERGENCIES IN THE ENVIRONMENT

Situation:

Person has fallen through ice into freezing water.

Actions:

- Try to reach the person from shore or give them something to grab onto from the shore, such as a stick, broom or rope. (You can tie something to the end of the rope and throw it to the person.)

- If that doesn't work, lie down on the ice to reach the person. This spreads your weight so the ice is less likely to crack under you.

- Once the person is holding on, you can pull them out. If you are grasping them directly, hold onto them by the wrists to pull them out.

- After you pull the person out of the water, get them out of wet clothing, dried off and warmed up.

DRILL SHEET FOR HANDLING EMERGENCIES IN THE ENVIRONMENT

EMERGENCIES IN NATURE

Tornado

Situation:

You are indoors and a tornado is coming.

Actions:

- Go to a storm cellar, a basement or a room or closet on the lowest floor, close to the center of the bilding.

- Stay away from windows.

- If possible, get under a heavy table.

- Cover your body with a blanket, coat or some other thick cloth to protect you from flying glass and be sure to protect your head.

DRILL SHEET FOR HANDLING EMERGENCIES IN THE ENVIRONMENT

Situation:

You are outdoors and a tornado is coming.

Actions:

- Lie down on the ground in the lowest place you can find.

- Cover your head and face with your arms.

- Do not hide under a bridge or overpass because the wind of the tornado is stronger in those places.

- Stay there until the tornado is over.

DRILL SHEET FOR HANDLING EMERGENCIES IN THE ENVIRONMENT

Earthquake

Situation:

An earthquake starts when you are indoors.

Actions:

- Stay away from windows.

- Get under a solid piece of furniture.

- Hang on so you don't get thrown from cover.

- Protect your head.

DRILL SHEET FOR HANDLING EMERGENCIES IN THE ENVIRONMENT

Situation

An earthquake starts when you are outdoors.

Actions:

- Get as far away as you can from buildings, power lines or other things that can fall on you.

- Crouch down and cover your head.

DRILL SHEET FOR HANDLING EMERGENCIES IN THE ENVIRONMENT

Situation

An earthquake starts when you are in a car.

Actions:

- Pull over and stop driving—but don't park on or under a bridge or overpass, as these can collapse.

- Stay in the car until the earthquake stops.

DRILL SHEET FOR HANDLING EMERGENCIES IN THE ENVIRONMENT

Flood

Situation:

Sudden flood

Actions:

- Get to higher ground without walking through moving water.

- If in a car and you can do it safely, leave the car and get to higher ground without walking through moving water.

DRILL SHEET FOR HANDLING EMERGENCIES IN THE ENVIRONMENT

Thunderstorm

Situation:

A thunderstorm starts near you.

Actions:

- If you can get to a building, go indoors, or get into a car.

- If you are in a car, stay there.

- If you are outdoors, move to the lowest point you can find.

- Crouch down and make yourself as small and low as possible, but touching the ground as little as possible. Don't lie on the ground.

www.ingramcontent.com/pod-product-compliance
Lightning Source LLC
Chambersburg PA
CBHW050502110426
42742CB00018B/3340